FROM MYTH TO HISTORY

The Acropolis and the goddess Athena

Text: Anastasia D. Makri
Illustrations: Michael Loukianos

Translated from Greek into English
Kiriaki Papakonstantinou

English Editor
Dr Nicola Wardle

Scientific consultant
Xanthi Proestaki
Dr of Archaeology and History of Art

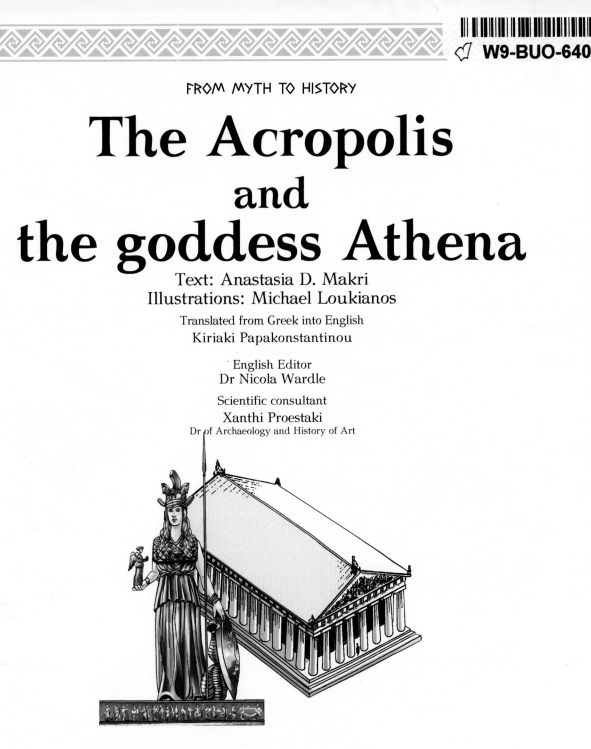

UNDER THE AEGIS OF

UNESCO
United Nations
Educational, Scientific
& Cultural Organization

CLUB FOR UNESCO OF THE DEPARTMENT OF PIRAEUS & ISLANDS
Petrou Ralli 210 & Thiseos 1 Nikea,
Tel.: 210 4967757, Fax: 210 4944564 - www.unescopireas.gr e-mail: unescop@otenet.gr

AGYRA
publications

Introduction

The ancient Greeks believed that this goddess had big, blue eyes. Her beauty was remarkable and her mind unmatched in its wisdom. She was the goddess Athena, the dearest daughter of all powerful Zeus, the father of all gods and men, who was born from her father's head.

This may seem rather strange and weird, but, in the world of the ancient gods and myth, anything could happen.

But, let us start at the beginning ...

Zeus was the son of Cronus and Rhea. Cronus was the leader of the Titans, the divine offspring of Gaia and Uranus. Cronus decided he wanted to seize power from his father, Uranus, so he challenged and defeated him - and so he became the leader of the Titans. Then he became afraid that his children would do the same to him! So when his wife Rhea gave birth to each of their children, he swallowed them. Rhea's tears and anguish were in vain; Cronus swallowed five children: Hestia, Demeter, Hera, Hades and Poseidon. But Rhea could not bear to lose her last child as she had the previous ones and when the time came to give birth, she went to Crete, to Mount Ida. There she gave birth to her last child, Zeus, giving him to the Nymphs to raise for his own protection.

When Zeus came of age, his mother told him what had happened to his siblings. Then, with the help of Metis, who later became his first wife, he gave his father an herb that made him expel all five children from his belly. This was how Zeus freed all his siblings.

Immediately after that, however, a war broke out between the Titans and the Olympians gods. This war was called the Titanomachy and lasted ten years. The victor in this war and consequently the absolute ruler of the whole world, was Zeus.

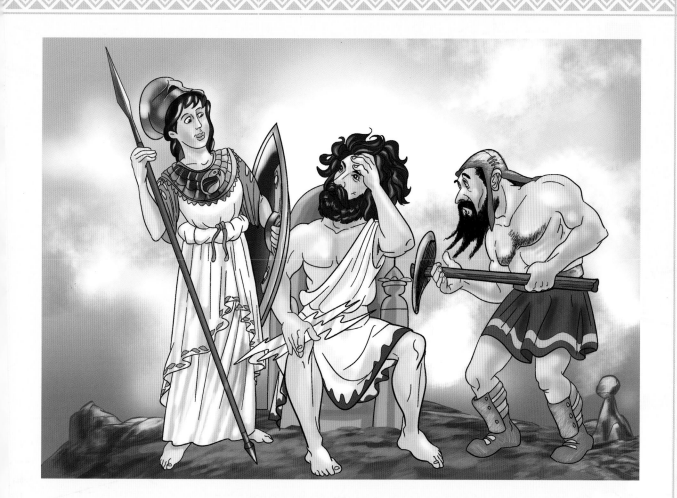

The Birth of Athena

The first wife of Zeus was the wise Metis. Metis was the daughter of Oceanus and Tethys. There was a prediction[1] given by the oracle saying that Metis would give birth first to a daughter and then to a son, who would rule gods and men. As soon as Zeus heard this his heart filled with sorrow. Immediately he asked for advice from Gaia and Uranus on what to do. They advised him to swallow his pregnant wife before she had the chance to give birth to their child. Zeus, whose fear of losing his power was greater than his love for his wife, followed their advice and swallowed the unfortunate Metis. Time passed and one day Zeus was tortured by an intolerable headache.

1. **Prediction:** an answer given by an Oracle to someone who asked for advice.

Unable to stand it for another minute, he called for his son, the god Hephaestus, and begged him for his help. Hephaestus grasped a hammer and hit Zeus hard on the head. What happened next left all the gods who were present speechless. Suddenly, from his head sprang Athena fully armed, with a war cry which shook the whole world. She wore a helmet and held a spear and shield, which she threw at Zeus' feet as a gesture of respect. Then, beautiful and imperious, she stood fearlessly in front of her father, who was proud that he was the one who had given birth to his daughter, rather than her mother, Metis.

Athena became Zeus' favourite daughter, and she was also one of the most beloved goddesses of the Ancient Greeks who respected her protection, courage and most of all her wisdom.

Thus, Athena became the goddess of wisdom, war and strategy. In addition, she was also the patron of the arts and taught mankind the art of pottery, woodworking, sculpture and weaving, as well as other crafts. Despite being the goddess of war, she hated violence and would rather help people to overcome their troubles. She actually assisted several heroes, such as Hercules, Jason and Odysseus – the last being Athena's favorite hero – to overcome numerous dangers. Her emblems were the owl, the cockerel and the aegis[1].

Athena and Medusa

Athena had placed the head of Medusa, also known as the Gorgon[2] on her shield. But, who was Medusa? She was a beautiful mermaid – a priestess who was loved by Poseidon. Medusa and Poseidon lay together in one of Athena's shrines. This made Athena angry with both of them. Reluctant, however, to take revenge on Poseidon, Athena directed her anger at Medusa. She transformed her into a horrible monster with venomous snakes for hair and cold eyes which would turn anyone who looked upon them into stone. Many had unsuccessfully tried to slay her, until the goddess Athena told Perseus, the famous hero, how Medusa could be killed: "When you attack her, do not look her in the eye, but look at her reflection in your shield" said the wise goddess. In this way, Perseus was successful. Not only did he kill Medusa, but he also cut off her head and gave it to Athena who put it on her shield.

---

1. **Aegis:** goat skin. Athena's aegis was made of the skin of the Chimera – a monstrous fire-breathing creature: part lion, part goat and part snake. The expression "under the aegis" means "under the protection of".
2. **Gorgon:** from "gorgos" meaning dreadful or terrible.

Athena and Pallas

Athena's best friend was the beautiful and brave nymph Pallas, who frequently competed against the goddess in spear throwing. Often the two of them pretended to fight a duel just to have fun. One day, however, they had a real quarrel. Pallas threw her spear directly at Athena's heart. Zeus, who was watching their duel unnoticed, out of fear for the life of his beloved daughter, immediately placed his shield in front of Athena to protect her. Pallas, startled, remained still and speechless. Then Athena, without a second thought struck her with her spear. The moment the beautiful nymph fell to the ground, Athena realised what she had done and threw herself onto her friend's lifeless body and

wept for the loss of her friend. Then, to sooth her sorrow, she fashioned a wooden statue (a xoanon) of her holding a spear in one hand and a distaff[1] in the other. This statue was called the Palladium and it was said to have been placed on Mount Olympus, beside the throne of Zeus. In this way she honoured her beloved friend, thus showing that she would never forget her ...

How her favourite city took the name of the goddess

The first mythical King of Athens was Cecrops[2]. During his reign, Attica was known as Cecropia. Cecrops was born from Mother Earth (Gaia). He was half man and half snake, with a serpent's tail instead of legs.

During the reign of King Cecrops, a dispute arose between Athena and Poseidon over who would become the patron of the city. Their dispute however, remained unresolved. Thus, they decided to appear before Cecrops on the Acropolis[3] and ask him to decide who should become the protector of the city. So, Cecrops asked each of them to offer a gift to the city.

First the god of the sea struck the rock with his trident and immediately salty water gushed forth. The gift symbolised the naval power that Poseidon could give to the city. Then, Athena struck the rock with her spear and a verdant green olive tree laden with fruit appeared. This tree, so valuable to the people for its olives and oil and a symbol of peace, was the gift of the goddess.

---

1. **Distaff:** a staff for holding the wool in spinning.
2. **Cecrops:** the first hero and king of Attica and a chthonic deity (of the underworld). He was worshipped on the Acropolis and he was depicted as a serpent-like creature.
3. **Acropolis:** from acro (edge) + polis (city). It means the highest point of the city.

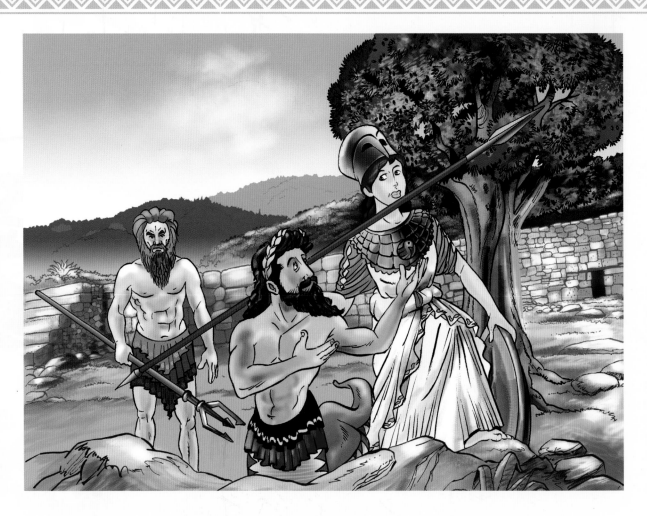

Without hesitation Cecrops chose Athena's gift. Thus, she became the patroness of the city which Erechtheus –a later king of Athens– named in honour of the goddess.

Athena and Arachne

Arachne was a famous weaver admired by many for her skill. She was, however, so proud of her own work that one day she went as far as to boast that her weaving was superior to that of the goddess Athena herself.

Athena was angry when she heard this. She appeared before Arachne and challenged her to a contest to produce the best piece of weaving. Both worked at their looms for days. When they had finished, they laid out their beautiful weaving for passersby to choose the best

one. Athena's tapestry depicted her dispute with Poseidon over the city of Athens, while Arachne's mocked the amorous adventures of the Olympian gods. When the goddess Athena saw it she was so angry that she immediately tore Arachne's weaving into pieces. Arachne felt so ashamed that she tried to hang herself. Athena, seeing her about to choke to death, felt pity for her and spared her life. She decided, however, to punish her, transforming her into an eight-legged spider which is where we get the name "arachnids" for all spiders. Ever since, the spider Arachne and her many offspring have spun beautiful webs...

Athena and Erichthonius

Athena never fell in love or wanted to marry. Nevertheless, the god Hephaestus once desired her. When he tried to embrace her, the goddess pushed him away angrily. Hephaestus' sperm, however, fell on her leg. Athena, enraged, wiped it off with a piece of wool which she threw on the ground. From this piece of wool and with the help of Gaia (Earth) Erichthonius was born – a creature half man and half snake.

The Panathenaea: a festival dedicated to goddess Athena

Athena loved the city of Athens, and the Athenians worshipped their patroness. To show their devotion, they organised an annual festival, the Panathenaea, with a Greater Panathenaea held every fourth year.

In the past, the residents of Athens had celebrated the "Athenea", but when the great hero Theseus became king of Athens and united all the towns of Attica the festival was renamed "the Panathenaea" – i.e. a festival for all residents of the towns around the capital of Athens. However, people from all over Greece would come to honour the goddess Athena.

The Greater Panathenaea, which was established by another leader of Athens,

the tyrant Peisistratos, lasted a whole week and included several athletic, musical, dance and theatrical contests, with prizes for the winners. However, the most important day of the festival was the last one, around the end of August in the modern calendar, when Athena's birthday was celebrated. Then the residents formed a large procession to carry the sacred peplos (a type of dress), which had been elaborately woven by young girls from the best Athenian families, called Ergastines[1], to the Acropolis where it would be dedicated to the goddess. The procession started in the Kerameikos[2] led by the priests, who accompanied a ship on wheels which had on its mast a cloth (like a sail) embroidered for Athena, followed by the Eragastines, the officials of Athens, nobles, etc. Following them were young men leading the animals to be sacrificed on the altar of Athena and young maidens carrying gifts and offerings for the goddess. Soldiers and horsemen followed and at the end were the residents of the city and all those who had travelled from far away just to honour their beloved goddess. When the procession arrived on the Acropolis the sacred peplos was put onto the wooden xoanon of the goddess Athena, the gifts were offered to the goddess, the animals were sacrificed on the altar, and the meat was consumed in an enormous banquet on the final night of the festival.

The first Acropolis

The first inhabitants of Athens built their houses on the summit of the Acropolis. The abundant springs at the foot of the rock, as well as its natural fortification, made the place suitable for settlement. Over the years, however, the population increased. Thus, they left the Acropolis and started building their homes on the slopes around

---

1. **Ergastines:** the maids who wove the sacred peplos for the goddess Athena.
2. **Kerameikos:** this area (to the NW of the Acropolis) was the potters' quarter of the city, from which the term "ceramic" is derived.

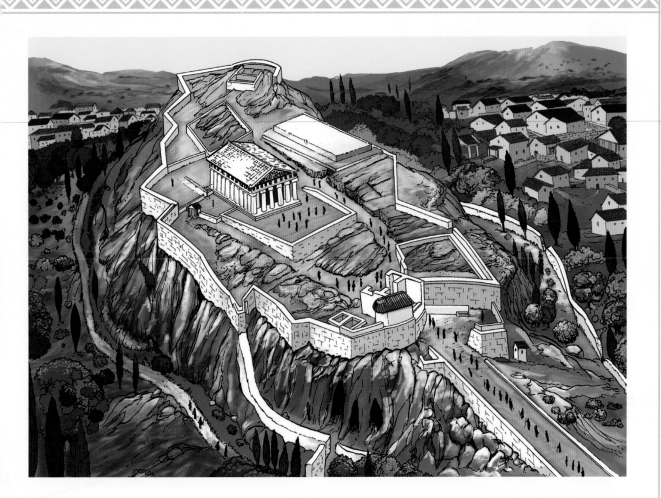

it. As for the Acropolis, it remained a sacred place, where the Greeks worshipped their gods, and most of all the goddess Athena, in the temples they had built there.

And so we come to the 6th century BC. The Athenians worshipped Athena in a small temple which had been built on the top of the Acropolis. At some point, however, they decided to build a bigger temple, the Hekatompedon, so-called because it measured 100 feet in length[1]. The Hekatompedon was the most important temple on the Acropolis at the end of the 6th century BC. It was located in the area now flanked by the Erechtheion and the Parthenon which were built later in the 5th century BC. In it was placed the ancient wooden xoanon of Athena Polias[2].

---

1. **Foot:** is a unit of length. One foot equals approximately 30 cm.
2. **Athena Polias:** one of the names of the goddess-protector of Athens and the Acropolis. (See also page 26).

However, in the year 490 BC Athens was in great peril. The Persians, who wanted to expand their country and acquire even more power, attacked Athens, but the Athenians resisted like lions to keep their homeland free and defeated the Persians at the battle of Marathon, despite their own much smaller army.

Ten years later, in 480 BC, the Persians attacked once more and conquered many cities including Athens and left behind many ruins. Among these ruins were the temples of the Acropolis, including an exquisite temple to Athena, construction of which had begun in gratitude to the goddess after the Athenian victory in 490 BC but was not yet finished. Eventually the Persians were defeated and the Athenians returned home. The Athenians, their hearts heavy with grief, decided to bury the ruined statues and offerings to their gods in large pits. For many years, their acropolis was to remain in ruins, but in time great masterpieces of art and culture would replace those bleak ruins.

5th century BC: the Golden Age

We are still in Athens, in the 5th century BC. One of the most significant events of the era was the emergence of democracy – a political system born in Greece and particularly in Athens. In Athenian democracy, all adult male citizens could express their viewpoints freely and participate by voting in decisions made concerning their city. This process was held at the Ekklesia of

the Demos[1]. From the middle of the 5th century BC, the leader of Athens was Pericles: an intelligent, educated man and a great orator[2] as well. He was a gifted statesman with big dreams for his home city. Actually, what's most striking about him is that he attempted to convince his fellow citizens how important it was to embellish the city where they lived and brought their children up. Thus, one of his dreams was to rebuild the temples on the Acropolis. This time its sanctuaries would be of unprecedented beauty. However, the greatest vision of this remarkable leader was to turn Athens into a cultural centre for all of Greece.

Important people and significant arts...

During this era of peace for the whole area, some rather important people lived in the city of Athens; educated and wise people who loved knowledge and tried to convince others of how important values such as justice and honesty were for their lives. Some of these great people were the philosopher[3] Socrates, whose thoughts and ideas still influence people around the world. Other important people were the historians Herodotus, also called the "father of History", and Thucydides. Furthermore, this was also the era of several painters and sculptors who created exquisite works of art still unsurpassed in craftsmanship and beauty.

Drama was another great passion of the ancient Greeks. Numerous masterpieces were written then and many are still

---

1. **Ekklesia of the Demos:** the assembly of the people in ancient Athens, in which all Athenian citizens participated in decision making concerning the city. Citizens of Athens were males whose parents were both born in Athens.
2. **Orator:** a person who can speak persuasively in public.
3. **Philosopher:** one who loves knowledge. Philosophy is s an activity people undertake when they seek to understand fundamental truths about themselves, the world in which they live, and their relationships to the world and to each other.

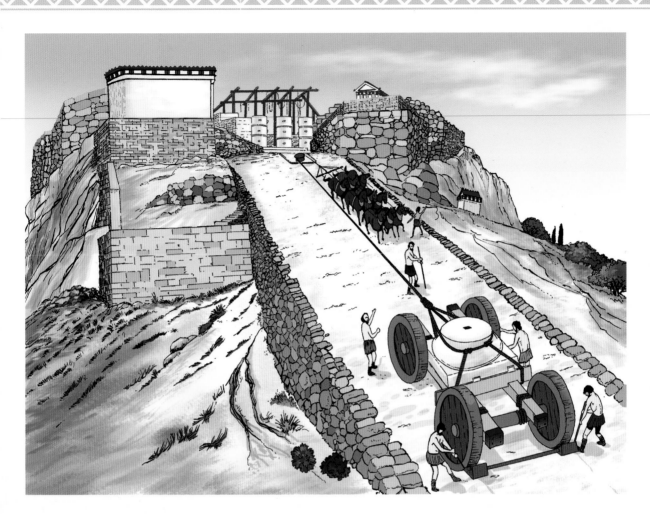

performed today. They invoked the admiration and respect of the audience not only in Greece but also in the whole world. These works were either painful tragedies or happy comedies that made their spectators laugh. Some of the great playwrights of that era were Aeschylus, Sophocles, Euripides and Aristophanes.

The Athenians agreed with Pericles' plan to rebuild the monuments of the Acropolis. Athens was the most powerful city in the whole of Greece; After its alliance[1] with some smaller city-states, Athens had undertaken their protection in return for payment. Thus, Athens could allocate a large part of the money from the alliance to fund the unique works of art created and established the Acropolis as a

---

1. **Alliance:** the Delian League, the alliance of smaller ancient Greek city-states under the leadership of Athens, with its headquarters on the island of Delos, was founded in 478 BC, initially with the aim to protect the city-states from the Persians.

symbol of civilization, unsurpassed in the whole world.

This period has been called "Classical", because of the unrivalled and timeless quality of the works of art created then. For the same reason, the century when Pericles lived and ruled was called "The Golden Age".

The dream comes true...

The moment you step foot on the top of the Acropolis, it is certain that apart from admiration you will be overwhelmed by the feeling of being transported to another world; a world where, above all, knowledge, honesty and respect were highly valued as well as the creativity which resulted in works of art and the improvement of everyday life.

All those works of art created on the Acropolis, still today go beyond capacity of human imagination. It is like a miracle.

But, let's go back in time once more, to see how all these monuments, which later went on to influence the whole of western culture, were created.

1. *Propylaea*
2. *Temple of Athena Nike*
3. *Pinakotheke*
4. *Peripatos*
5. *Athena Promachos*
6. *Arrephoreion*
7. *Erechtheion*
8. *Parthenon*
9. *Temple of Rome and Augustus*

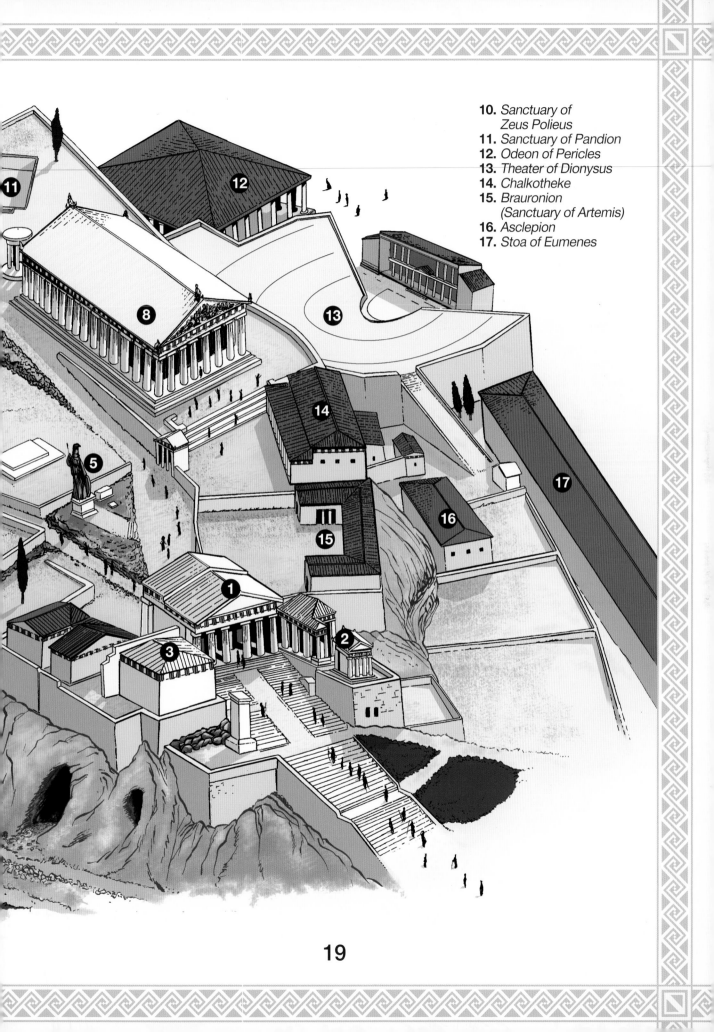

10. *Sanctuary of
    Zeus Polieus*
11. *Sanctuary of Pandion*
12. *Odeon of Pericles*
13. *Theater of Dionysus*
14. *Chalkotheke*
15. *Brauronion
    (Sanctuary of Artemis)*
16. *Asclepion*
17. *Stoa of Eumenes*

The Parthenon

The sculptor Phidias, an extremely talented artist, was a good friend of Pericles. Thus, he was the one commissioned by Pericles to supervise the first and most significant project: the construction of the Parthenon.

The temple derived its name from its dedication to Athena Parthenos. The great architects of this project were Ictinus and Callicrates. The construction of the temple started in 447 BC and continued until 438 BC. Given its size and sophistication it was built in a remarkably short time. Builders, marble workers, sculptors and painters worked tirelessly on this unique project. Then Phidias with his pupils undertook to decorate it with wonderful sculptures[1]. The most elaborate and beautiful was the chryselephantine statue[2] of the goddess Athena which was placed in the sekos[3] of the temple. Inside the sekos, a two-storey colonnade[4] formed the Greek letter Pi (Π). A sculpted marble frieze[5] ran around the top of the outer walls of the sekos; a clearly

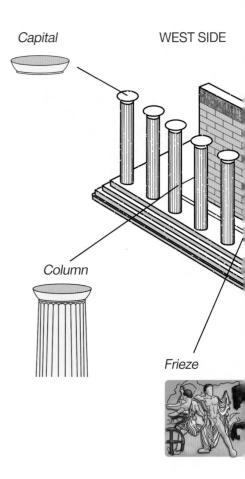

Capital   WEST SIDE

Column

Frieze

---

1. **Sculpture:** 3D depiction of a figure or scene in marble, gold, copper, etc.
2. **Statue:** the Greek word *agalma* derives from the ancient verb *aggalomai,* which means *be pleased with.* The ancient Greeks dedicated sculptures to the gods to please them. That's why they were called *agalmata* = statues.
3. **Sekos or cella:** the central part of the temple where the statue of a deity was placed.
4. **Colonnade:** a row of evenly spaced columns supporting a roof.
5. **Frieze:** the long zone above the columns decorated with a series of scenes of humans and animals.

The Parthenon is a peripteral octastyle Doric temple. It is of post and lintel construction and is surrounded by columns ("peripteral") carrying an entablature. There are eight columns at either end ("octastyle") and seventeen on the sides. Each column is 10.5 meters high and is made of pure white Pentelic marble. Outside the temple there were pediments[1], statues and metopes[2] decorated with brightly painted reliefs[3]. The Parthenon was also the place where the funds of the treasury of the Delian League were kept.

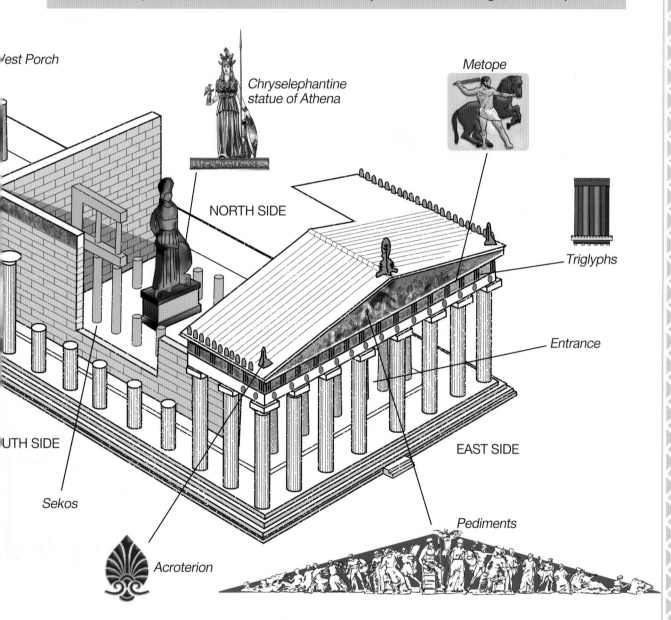

West Porch

Chryselephantine statue of Athena

Metope

NORTH SIDE

Triglyphs

Entrance

SOUTH SIDE

EAST SIDE

Sekos

Pediments

Acroterion

---

1. **Pediments:** the triangular gable forming the end of the roof over a portico. The pediment was the crowning feature of the front of a temple and was often decorated with sculpture.
2. **Metopes:** rectangular slabs: early examples were painted and later ones carved which, along with the triglyphs, form the frieze.
3. **Reliefs:** scenes carved on slabs of marble, metal, etc. as if emerging from the background.

Ionic[1] element in a Doric[2] temple. The 12m high statue was made of gold and ivory. In her right hand she held a winged Nike (Victory) and in her left a shield.

The east pediment depicts the birth of Athena. The statues of Zeus, Hephaestus and Athena were placed at the centre while the sculptures of other gods, seated as if watching, were arranged on each side. At one end of the pediment, represented by the heads of horses, is the chariot of the Moon setting and on the other end the chariot of the Sun rising, marking in this way the time Athena was born.

In the centre of the west pediment, stood Poseidon with his trident and Athena with her spear. This illustrates the conflict between the two gods over who would become the patron of the city. At either end two figures represent rivers in Athens thus

1. **Ionic:** order of architecture which first appeared on the coast of Ionia of Asia Minor, the islands of the Aegean Sea and Attica. An order characterized by light construction and rich décor.
2. **Doric:** another order of Classical architecture characterized by rigor and simplicity.

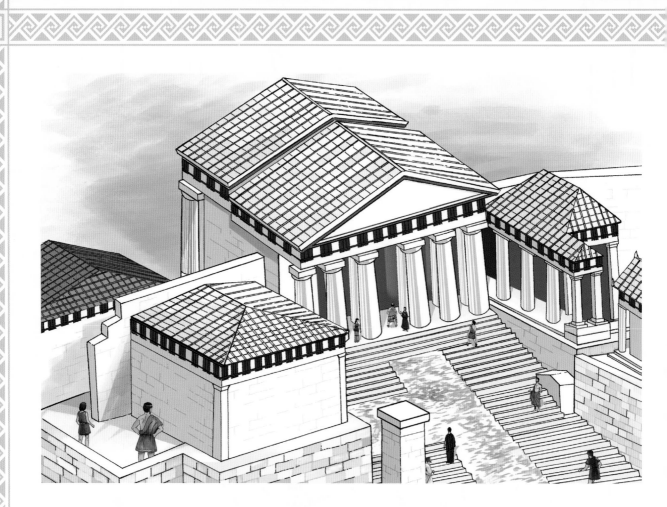

setting the geographical location. The mythical king Cecrops, the gods and heroes were spectators of the scene.

The reliefs on the metopes of the temple depict scenes from legend, such as the Trojan War, the Battle between the Lapiths and the Centaurs, between the gods and the giants, as well as between the Greeks and the Amazons. The festival of the Great Panathenaea is depicted on the east end of the Parthenon frieze.

The Propylaea

When the construction of the Parthenon was completed, the Propylaea was built at the entrance of the Acropolis. The Propylea was an impressive building built in Pentelic marble. In ancient times it was approached via a flight of stairs leading to the temples of the Acropolis, with rooms on the right and left. Mnesikles was the architect of the project. The left room housed the Pinakotheke, which accommodated works of the great painter Polygnotus. This was the first picture gallery (= pinakotheke in Greek) in the world. The Propylea was never completed because of the war that broke out between the Athenians and Spartans. This war, known as the Peloponnesian War, started in 431 BC and lasted until 404 BC. In 429 BC, during the war, Pericles died from the plague[1] that ravaged the city. Nevertheless, the projects on the Acropolis continued. Thus, two new temples of exquisite artistry took their place on the Acropolis ...

The Temple of Athena Nike

Beside the Propylea a beautiful, small temple of Athena Nike (Victory) was built in the Ionic style. During the Roman period it was known as the Temple of Nike Apteros (Wingless) and the absence of wings

---

1. **Plague:** the Athenian plague was a highly contagious disease.

on the statue has been interpreted as the desire by the Athenians that Nike should never leave their city. The architect of the temple, the construction of which began in 427 BC, was Callicrates. Inside the sekos, there was a statue of Athena Nike with a helmet in one hand and a pomegranate in the other. The pomegranate was a symbol of the gods of the underworld.

The Erechtheion or the Temple of Athena Polias

The construction of this temple started in 420 BC. The Ancient Greeks believed that the temple was built at the spot where Athena and Poseidon had their conflict over who would become the patron of the city. They also believed it was the palace of the legendary king Erechtheus, after whom it is named. In the Erechtheion, besides Athena, the Athenians also worshipped Poseidon, Hephaestus, Cecrops - the first mythical king of the city - as well as the local heroes Erechtheus and Voutis[1]. Next to the temple grew the sacred olive tree, the gift of goddess Athena. The most famous

---

1. **Voutis:** the twin brother of king Erechtheus and a priest of Poseidon.

part of the temple is the south porch, the roof of which is supported by six beautiful statues, the famous Caryatids[1], guardians of the tomb of Erechtheus. Among the dedications to the temple, was the 7m high bronze statue of Athena, created by Phidias, which could be seen from afar. The construction of the temple finished between 407 and 406 BC.

Lord Elgin and the Parthenon Marbles

In 1799, when Greece was under Ottoman occupation, the Scottish noble Thomas Bruce, the Seventh Earl of Elgin, was appointed ambassador in Constantinople. He acquired a firman (a license) from the Sultan, giving him permission to study the sculptures of the Parthenon

---

1. **Caryatids (Korai):** sculpted female figures taking the place of a column or a pillar supporting an entablature on their head.

for reasons of artistic license and to remove fragments as necessary. Elgin, while in Constantinopole, engaged his chaplain Hunt to remove parts of the Parthenon sculptures and have them shipped to Britain, where he sold them to the British Museum, after a special meeting of the British government. Today, the Parthenon Marbles are on exhibition in the British Museum and Greece is seeking, via diplomatic channels to have them returned home, where they belong...

Other buildings and sanctuaries

In addition to the four major monuments on the Acropolis – the Parthenon, the Erechtheion, the Temple of Athena Nike and the Propylaea, other buildings and sanctuaries were also built:

The Brauronion, dedicated to goddess Artemis, patroness of women in labour. It was probably a dependency of the big sanctuary at Brauron in Attica which was built in the shape of the Greek letter Pi (Π).

The Arrephoreion: a square building which housed the two Arrephores, the two young girls chosen each year to weave the peplos of the goddess Athena.

Chalkotheke

29

Odeon of Pericles

The Chalkotheke: the place where the bronze offerings to the goddess Athena were kept.

On the south slopes below the Acropolis stood the **Odeon of Pericles,** the **Asclepion** – dedicated to Asclepius, the god of medicine – and the **Theatre of Dionysus,** one of the earliest theatres in the world.

The **Sanctuary of Zeus Polieus:** where the sacrifices of oxen took place during the festival of Diipolion. In the Archaic period, oxen were fed nearby.

The **Sanctuary of Pandion:** Dedicated to the mythical king and hero Pandion, son of Erichthonius or Cecrops. The old museum of the Acropolis stands nowadays on its ruins.

In addition, the whole area between temples was full of statues and inscriptions all dedicated to the goddess Athena by the faithful. Many of these are now exhibited in the new Acropolis Museum.

The new Acropolis Museum
A short tour

The New Acropolis Museum opened to the public in June 2009. The museum is located 300m from the Acropolis in Makriyanni, an historic district of Athens. It was built deliberately in direct line of sight with the Acropolis – especially from the room where the Parthenon sculptures are exhibited. The glass sides of the room give visitors the chance to enjoy the magnificent view of the surrounding historic hills. The museum provides an ideal shelter for all the precious finds from the area around the Acropolis, with finds dating from prehistoric times to the early Christian period.

On entering the ground floor lobby of the museum, one notices a glass-floored gallery. The remains of part of the ancient city, discovered during the construction of the building, can be seen through this floor.

Then, there is the first hall of the museum, the "Gallery of the Slopes of the Acropolis", which presents finds from the slopes of the Acropolis. These are the finds from the settlement and the sanctuaries located there.

On the first floor is the "Archaic Gallery" hosting the sculptures that adorned the large early temples of the Acropolis, as well as the offerings of the faithful: Korai[1], Kouroi[2], terracotta and bronze figurines[3], hippeis[4], scribes, statues of the goddess Athena, marble reliefs, pottery and other small bronze offerings.

The third level accommodates the "Parthenon Gallery". Here, the marble slabs of the frieze depicting the Panathenaic procession are depicted. The metopes, carved with mythological scenes, have been installed between the steel columns equal in number to the columns of the Parthenon. The two pediments are also there: the east one depicting the birth of Athena from the head of Zeus and the west pediment depicting the conflict over the city between Athena and Poseidon.

Then the visitor descends back to the first floor, where parts of the Propylaea, the Temple of Athena Nike and the Erechtheion are exhibited. There, one has the opportunity of a unique view of the sculptures of the classical period, Roman copies, offerings

---

1. **Kore:** a type of Archaic statue depicting a standing female figure in a rigid pose draped in a variety of clothes and featuring the characteristic mysterious smile.
2. **Kouros:** a type of Archaic statue depicting a male figure standing naked, with arms close to the body, the clenched hands securely attached to the thighs and featuring the characteristic mysterious smile.
3. **Figurine:** in marble, clay or metal, depicting an abstract or concrete form of a human, animal, or object.
4. **Hippeis:** statues of horsemen, probably dedicated by the respective social class of horsemen or charioteers.

and reliefs of the 5th and 4th centuries BC, as well as sculpted pedestals of statues and portraits. Furthermore, selected works of late antiquity and early Byzantine period are also exhibited there.

Each visitor to these unique sites, both outside and inside the museum, feels the significance of such monuments. Also, one understands the reason why the civilisation and art of that era had a positive cultural impact across the globe. Perhaps, one feels that people can improve, mainly through literature and art, the values of mutual respect and peace.

Useful Information

The Acropolis over time

The passage of time has caused less damage to this remarkable monument than man.

Towards the end of the Roman period the ancient Olympian gods began to go out of fashion. By the end of the rule of the Byzantine Emperor Constantine the Great (AD 306-337), Christianity had become the official religion of the Byzantine Empire. The Parthenon was converted into a church dedicated to Virgin Mary; the Propylaea into a church of the Archangels and the Erechtheion became the church of the Theotokos (Holy Mary, Mother of Jesus).

Later followed the Frankish period (AD 1204-1566). The Frankish rulers chose the Acropolis as their residence. Eventually, when the Turks occupied Athens (AD 1456) the Parthenon became a mosque and parts of the Acropolis were used to store gunpowder. In AD 1655 a lightning strike destroyed the Propylaea. As if this was not enough, the Turks pulled down the Temple of Athena Nike to construct a gun implacement.

The most significant damage, however, was caused in 1687 by the bombardment of the Acropolis by the Venetian Commander-in-Chief Morosini, who was fighting against the Turks. During the siege of the Acropolis, he scored a direct hit on the Parthenon which the defending Turks were using as a storage magazine for their gunpowder. The explosion destroyed the temple. Then, after occupying the Acropolis, he plundered many of the treasures that remained. The next major event in its history was the removal of the Parthenon Marbles by Lord Elgin.

After the liberation of Greece from the Turks, restoration and maintenance started on the monuments that remained on the Acropolis. This work continues today...

Did you know that...

- The Parthenon has been on the list of UNESCO world cultural heritage sites since September 11th, 1987.

- Not all the original sculptures which adorned the pediments are in the New Acropolis Museum. Many fragments of the originals are housed in the British Museum, some in the Louvre and other museums in Europe. The copies are in a different colour.

34

- Music and dance played a very important role in the lives of the Ancient Greeks. They would play music and dance during any significant event, such as religious celebrations, weddings, etc.

- A chisel was the tool used by sculptors to carve marble or wood.

- The offerings people dedicated to Athena on the Acropolis depended on their wealth and status. The rich would offer marble statues, sculptures, and bronze items, while the poor would offer clay figurines and reliefs.

- The Acropolis housed many more female statues than male ones, as the offerings were for a female deity, the goddess Athena.

- The huge amount of gold (more than two thousand pounds) Phidias used in the construction of the chryselephantine statue of Athena, gave his enemies the opportunity to accuse him of stealing the gold. Phidias, however, had actually assembled the golden garment of the statue in such a way that he could remove the pieces of gold and weigh them. The gold weighed exactly the amount he had been paid by the Delion League. So, Phidias proved his innocence.

- The statue of Zeus at Olympia is another of Phidias' creations and was one of the Seven Wonders of the Ancient World. He was commissioned to create the statue for the temple of Zeus at Olympia.

The most common epithets of the goddess Athena

Pallas: perhaps because she killed the giant Pallas during the Gigantomachy or, because when she was born from the head of Zeus her spear *"epalle"* (= pulsated).

Glafkopis: often used by the poet Homer, meaning blue-eyed. Also, the ancient Greek name of the owl, the sacred bird of Athena, is glauka. It comes from the same root. This may be due to the fact that the owl also has large and bright eyes.

Ergane: (= weaver) because she was the patroness of arts and crafts.

Promachos: because she entered battle fully armed.

Polias: because she was considered the patroness of the city and the Acropolis.

Parthenos: because she never wanted a partner.

How well do you know the Acropolis?

Can you remember and write down the names of buildings, monuments and sanctuaries of Acropolis?

1. ....

2. ....

3. ....

4. ....

5. ....

6. ....

7. ....

8. ....

9. ....

10. ....

11. ....

12. ....

13. ....

14. ....

15. ....

16. ....

17. ....

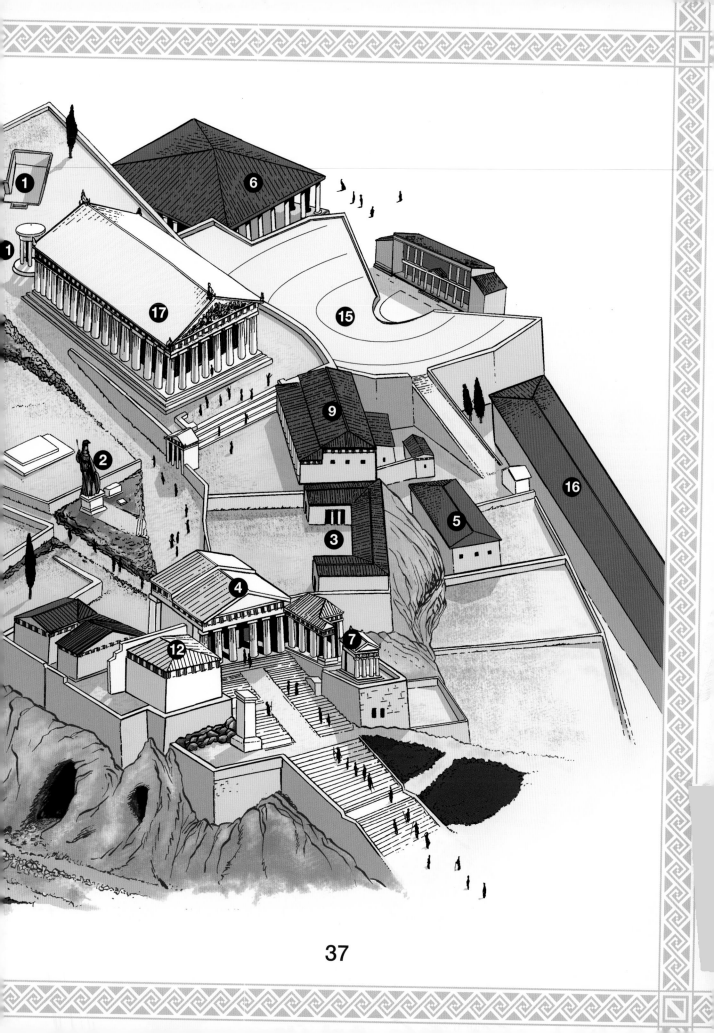

Wordsearch

Can you find the 9 words in each wordsearch from the list below?

1. GOLDEN AGE
2. THUCYDIDES
3. PALLAS
4. PANATHENAEA
5. ARISTOPHANES
6. SOCRATES
7. ARACHNE
8. PERICLES
9. CECROPS
10. AESCHYLUS
11. PHIDIAS
12. MEDUSA
13. EURIPIDES
14. PERSEUS
15. ERICHTHONIUS
16. KERAMEIKOS
17. HERODOTUS
18. HEKATOMPEDON

A	V	S	I	J	H	U	K	L	N	Y	C	M	Y	P
T	G	O	L	D	E	N	A	G	E	B	F	X	H	Z
I	M	C	S	O	K	P	E	O	U	Q	G	J	K	U
E	H	R	C	P	A	S	P	E	R	I	C	L	E	S
B	Q	A	L	J	T	F	A	M	I	H	U	M	R	U
L	G	T	A	N	O	K	L	R	P	B	Y	L	A	K
A	R	E	O	D	M	B	L	O	I	N	I	D	M	Z
R	Y	S	U	H	P	O	A	Q	D	S	H	Y	E	A
A	P	E	F	K	E	X	S	D	E	L	G	U	I	S
C	O	I	N	L	D	I	H	O	S	T	X	B	K	N
H	E	R	O	D	O	T	U	S	R	C	I	O	O	R
N	K	M	N	V	N	I	S	U	K	M	Y	P	S	H
E	L	Y	A	K	S	P	G	Z	J	Q	E	M	O	Y
O	Y	C	J	R	I	L	V	K	X	A	L	U	G	L

P	O	A	E	S	C	H	Y	L	U	S	K	J	Y	N
E	G	H	R	M	Q	K	T	N	Y	G	H	D	L	T
S	B	P	I	L	C	H	K	U	F	X	M	S	Q	H
P	N	J	C	D	A	P	B	P	J	H	O	P	K	U
A	O	E	H	F	V	A	J	H	T	M	F	E	P	C
N	I	R	T	L	H	Q	F	I	C	E	U	R	N	Y
A	J	T	H	O	U	C	R	D	I	D	E	S	H	D
T	D	P	O	G	N	E	P	I	N	U	Y	E	I	I
H	K	C	N	O	H	C	D	A	R	S	M	U	J	D
E	B	U	I	F	K	R	L	S	S	A	Z	S	A	E
N	I	M	U	Q	I	O	J	O	C	V	E	Z	M	S
A	R	I	S	T	O	P	H	A	N	E	S	B	K	G
E	P	G	O	D	P	S	S	F	G	Y	I	L	Z	X
A	L	A	K	F	N	X	E	V	J	O	C	T	N	B